MW00950523

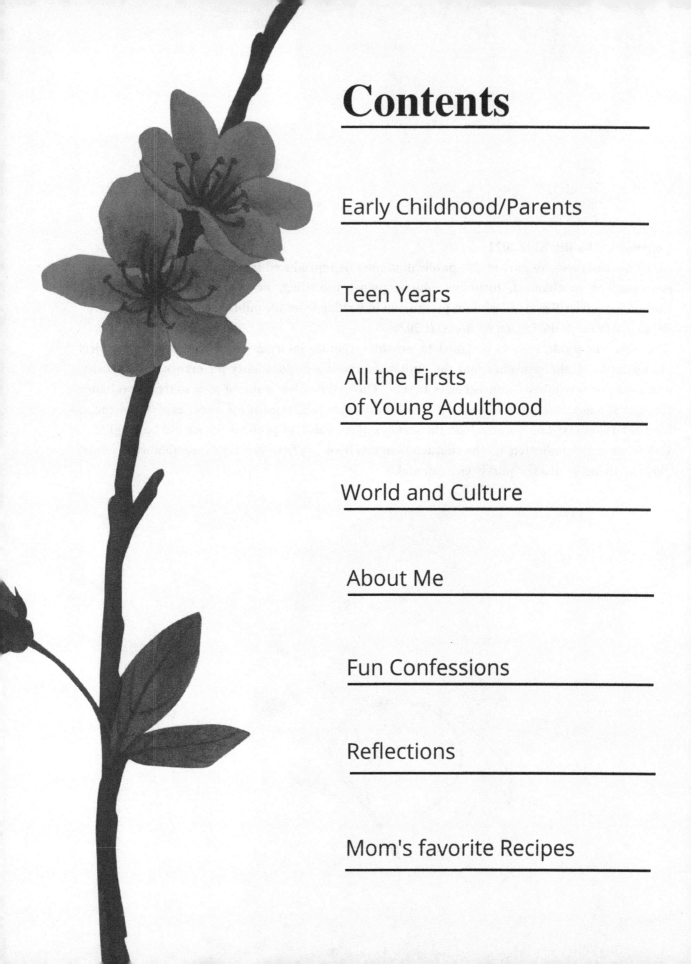

Contents

This book belongs to:

"Mothers are like glue. Even when you can't see them, they're still holding the family together." —Susan Gale

HER·STORY

Born on

City of Birth

Parents

Siblings

Profession

Spouse

Children

Faith

Early Childhood & Parents

How would you describe your mother's personality?

What did she do for a Living?

How would you describe your father's personality?

What did he do for a Living?

How would you describe your personality through life?

Childhood

As an adult

Now

How would your parents have described you?

What was your relationship like with your parents?
Were they strict?

How was the financial situation at home when you were a child?

Describe the neighborhood you grew up in...

Did you have any pets growing up? What were they? What were their names?

Who was your closest friend growing up? What happened to him/her?

What was your dream job when you were a kid?

What was your favorite thing to eat for breakfast? Who made it?

Were you close to your grandparents? What was one of your best memories of them?

Favorite family tradition/holiday when you were young... What was it? How did you celebrate?

What values were stressed in your home?

What types of mischief did you and your siblings get into? How would you describe your siblings personalities back then?

What was the best piece of advice you were given by your mom/dad?

What kinds of games did you play on the Schoolyard?

Additional Questions/Notes

Teen Years

When you were a teenager, what was the price of:

A new car $_____

A house $_____

A gallon of gas $_____

A dozen eggs $_____

A loaf of bread $_____

Were you a part of any club/band in high school? What was it? Which instrument did you play?

What was your favorite hangout spot in high school?

What was your favorite subject/class in school?

Who was your favorite actor growing up?

What was one thing you were insecure about as a teen?

What was the most annoying rule your parents gave when you were a teenager?

What is the one piece of advice you would give your teenage self?

Did you have a curfew as a teenager? What time was it? What happened if you missed it?

What were the most popular dances? Could you do them?

Were you allowed to wear short skirts or make-up?

What genre of music did you and all your friends listen to?

What is the one technology or gadget you wish was available when you were a teenager?

What is the biggest difference between teenagers today and teenagers during your time?

Slang! What were some popular words or phrases when you were a teen? And what are the meanings?

Slang! What were some popular words or phrases when you were a teen? And what are the meanings?

Additional Questions/Notes

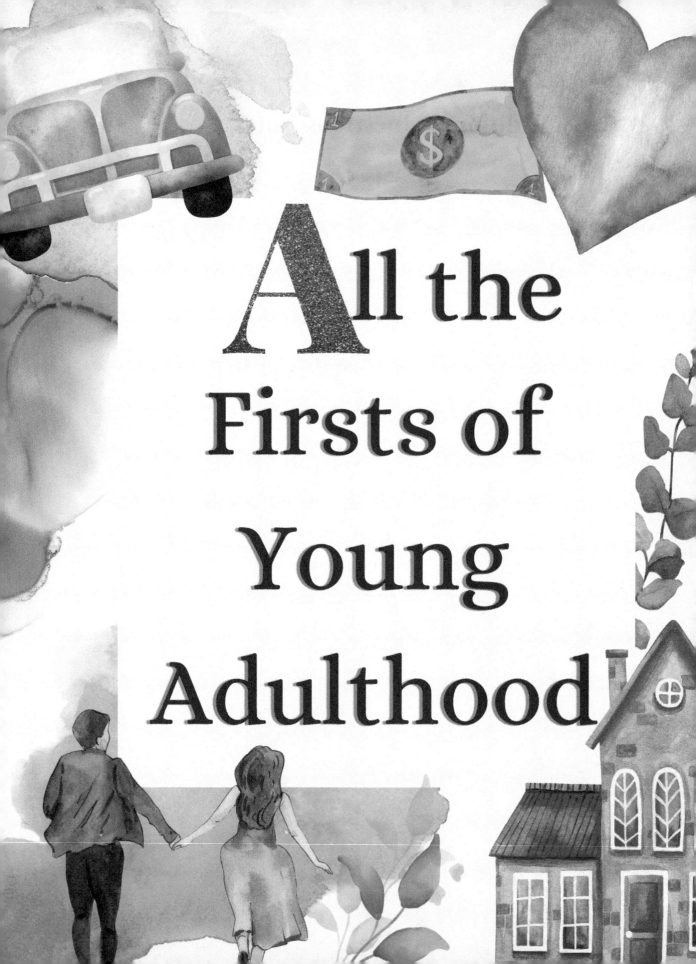

All the Firsts of Young Adulthood

What was your first job, and how much were you paid?

How did you spend your first paycheck?

Who taught you to drive?

When did you buy your first car? How did you pay for it? What was it? What happened to it?

Where did you meet your first love? How old were you?

How old were you when you had your first kiss? Did you tell your parents?

How did you realize you wanted to spend the rest of your life with your spouse?

What was the highlight of your wedding day?

Did you go on a honeymoon? Where?

Describe your first house/apartment…

Was there ever a time when you moved back in with your parents after being on your own?

Additional Questions/Notes

World and Culture

What was it like growing up in (city)_____ during the (decade) _____?

What was the worst decade for fashion? What were the worst trends, and did you copy them?

What were some common ways that teens would assert their independence when you were growing up?

What, would you say is the worst thing about our society today? What is the best?

How do you feel about... Religion?

Politics?

Additional Questions/Notes

About Me

How did you feel when you first learned you were pregnant?

How was I as a baby? Was I a difficult baby to manage?

Were there any disagreements between you and my dad about parenting children?

What did you feel when you first saw me after I was born?

What is your favorite memory about me?

What was the most annoying thing about me when I was little?

According to you, whom do I resemble the most personality-wise?

What was the most challenging thing about being a parent to two/three/four children?

Did I walk first or talk first? What was my first word?

What was the most embarrassing thing any of us (your child/children) did in public?

Additional Questions/Notes

Fun
Confessions

Have you ever acted sick to skip school?

When did you first consume alcohol?

Have you ever gotten in trouble with the law?

Did your parents ever catch you smoking or drinking when you were a teen?

What was the most embarrassing thing your parents have ever said to you in front of your friends?

Have you ever met a celebrity? Who was it? What was it like?

What is the wildest thing you've ever done? Did you regret it later? Why?

Additional Questions/Notes

Reflection

How many times have you fallen in love?

What was the worst job you ever had? What was so bad about it?

What was the best job you ever had? Why did you leave?

In what way was your upbringing different from mine?

What was your biggest belief about raising children that turned out to be untrue?

What is the biggest life lesson your parents have taught you?

How did you change as a person after having children?

If you had a chance to change anything about the way you raised children, what would you change?

Do you think your experiences as a child impacted the way you raised and disciplined me/us?

What is something that you once resented your parents for, but later grew to appreciate?

Is there any member of your family you wish I had met? Why?

Who did you admire most while growing up?

What was the most difficult habit to break, or obstacle you had to overcome? How did you do it?

What do you wish your parents had taught you before you learned the hard way?

What is the one mistake you made that you never want me to make?

What are you most grateful for in life?

What was the most difficult phase of your life?

Besides me, what would you say is your biggest accomplishment?

What is one thing you wish you'd learned to do when you were younger?

How do you want the world to remember you?

What was the most fun time period in your life?

Additional Questions/Notes

Favorites!

Favorite Song/Album

Favorite Color

Favorite Book

Favorite Movie or TV Show

Other Favorites!

One of Mom's favorite Recipes

Recipe for: _____

One of Mom's favorite Recipes

Recipe for: _____

One of Mom's favorite Recipes

Recipe for: _____

One of Mom's favorite Recipes

Recipe for: _____

One of Mom's favorite Recipes

Recipe for: _____

One of Mom's favorite Recipes

Recipe for: _____

Additional Questions/Notes

Additional Questions/Notes

Additional Questions/Notes

Additional Questions/Notes

Additional Questions/Notes

Additional Questions/Notes

Made in the USA
Las Vegas, NV
23 December 2024